Trees

Esmond Harris

Illustrated by
Bob Bampton & Josephine Martin

Piccolo
A Piper Book

Contents

Introduction   3
Looking at Trees   4
Leaves   6
Flowers and Seeds   8
How a Tree Grows   10
Other Things to Do   12
Finding Out More About Trees   13

IDENTIFICATION SECTION
Coniferous Trees   14
Broad-leafed Trees   24
Unusual Trees   45

Index   48

Edited by Angela Royston
Illustrated by Bob Bampton and Josephine Martin/
The Garden Studio

Introduction  *Raksha.*

Trees are all around us, in the countryside and in towns too. The more you know about them the more interesting they become. This book shows the trees you are most likely to see and one or two unusual ones as well. There is space for you to record when and where you first saw the tree and its girth. From the girth you can estimate the age of the tree (see page 11). Only trees are shown here, not shrubs. Trees have a single main trunk. Shrubs from several woody stems grow from ground level.

Native trees are those that were growing here before people started to farm the land. They now grow mainly in woods and hedges. Trees from other parts of the world are often planted in Britain as a large number grow well here. They are grown for their showy flowers or attractive autumn colours and bark, and because they do not get too large in small gardens and near buildings. Trees from warmer climates can often grow in towns where pavements and buildings reflect the sunlight and the buildings provide warmth.

Trees in towns may need to be cut back or replaced fairly frequently so that their roots do not damage buildings nor their branches keep the light from windows. In the countryside much larger trees, like our native oaks and beech, can be allowed to grow for much longer. Some may well be over a hundred years old, but they too can become dangerous if left too long. Younger trees should be encouraged to come up ready to replace them. Look for the tiny seedlings under large trees and notice how they will grow tall when there is sufficient light coming through the upper branches for them.

Some of our large woodland trees were brought to Britain many hundreds of years ago and have become naturalized. This means they now grow naturally here, producing lots of seedlings. Sycamore and sweet chestnut are two examples of naturalized trees.

Looking at Trees

There are two main groups of trees – conifers and broad-leafed trees.

Conifers have cones and needle-like or scale-like leaves which may stay on the trees for several years. Broad-leafed trees have much larger, flatter leaves which usually fall in the autumn leaving the trees bare in winter. They often turn brilliant red or yellow before falling.

To identify a tree, decide first whether it is a conifer or a broad-leafed tree. Remember that not all evergreen trees are conifers, nor all conifers evergreen. In spring and summer the leaves may be the most obvious way to recognize a tree, but look at the bark, the fruit and the shape of the tree as well. They are all important clues. In winter look too for seeds which have fallen under the tree and at the buds on the twigs.

BARK

Practise recognizing a tree from its bark. Look closely at the details. Here are four examples.

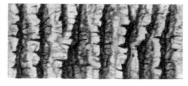

Ridged bark like that of oak.

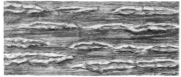

Banded bark like the cherry.

Stringy bark like that of redwoods.

Smooth bark like that of beech.

GLOSSARY

Bract scale Thin scale growing between each cone scale.
Catkin Long, hanging flower without coloured petals.
Cone Woody fruit containing seeds on coniferous trees.
Cone scale Scale on the cone stalk holding the seeds.
Flower A specialized part of the tree for making seeds.
Fruit A fleshy or woody body containing ripe seeds.
Hybrid A tree arising from two different species of tree.
Leaflet The separate part of a divided leaf.
Leaf scar Mark left on twig where the leaf has fallen off.
Native Growing here naturally before introduction began.
Naturalized Introduced from abroad but now growing naturally.
Needle Name given to the narrow leaf of some conifers.
Nut A seed with a hard coat containing stored food.
Seed Product of the flower from which new seedlings grow.
Sucker A shoot from a root that grows into a new tree.
Variety An unusual or slightly different form of a tree.
Veins Tubes in leaves that carry sap and water.

WINTER TWIGS

Buds form on the twigs in late summer and knowing this may help you to identify the trees in winter.

Beech has shiny brown, pointed buds and rich brown twigs.

Oak has rounded buds, clustered at the tip and grey-green bark.

Larch has round buds and leaf bases on yellow twigs.

Sycamore has green buds and leaf scars on brown twigs.

Ash has black angular buds and shiny grey-green bark.

Hawthorn has little round buds and long sharp thorns.

Leaves

MAIN LEAF SHAPES

Leaves are the easiest part of the tree to identify. The main shapes are shown below. Simple leaves may be rounded, oval, triangular or long. They may have toothed or smooth edges or they may be lobed. Compound leaves may be hand-shaped or feather-shaped. Conifers have needle-like leaves or scale-like leaves.

How many of the leaves shown below can you identify?

HOW LEAVES GROW

Look at the way leaves grow on the twig. Leaves which grow in pairs are called opposite. Leaves which grow first on one side of the twig, then on the other, are called alternate. The needles of conifers grow in a spiral. They may grow as single needles in groups or in rosettes.

As you will see, some leaves grow as big as 80 cm while others are only 1 mm long. Consequently, they are not drawn to scale.

SIMPLE LEAVES

Rounded

Triangular

Lobed

Long

COMPOUND LEAVES

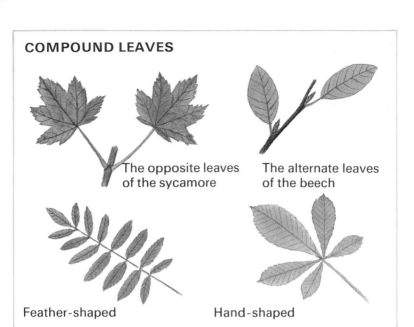

The opposite leaves of the sycamore

The alternate leaves of the beech

Feather-shaped

Hand-shaped

CONIFERS

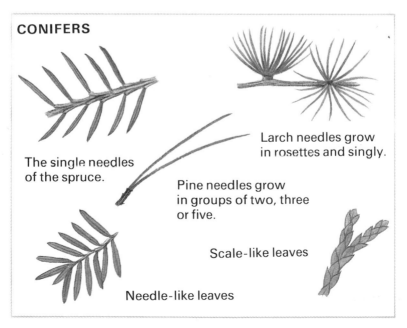

Larch needles grow in rosettes and singly.

The single needles of the spruce.

Pine needles grow in groups of two, three or five.

Scale-like leaves

Needle-like leaves

Flowers and Seeds

All trees have flowers, including conifers, but the latter are small and often high up in the tree, so they may not be easy to see.

Male flowers produce yellow pollen which fertilizes the female flower and this results in the formation of seeds. On some kinds of tree the male and female parts are in the same flower, on others they are in separate flowers and some occur on separate male and female trees. For example, only some holly trees have berries and these are the female trees.

The seeds produced are protected by a soft fruit on some kinds of trees and by a hard nut on others. Conifer seeds are always contained in cones.

Look out for the various types of seeds with their different coverings and note down where you find them.

FLOWERS

The female flower of the Douglas fir. Conifers always have separate male and female flowers, usually on the same tree.

The male and female catkins of the willow. Pollen is blown from the yellow male flowers on to the green female flowers.

The sweet chestnut catkin has many male flowers at the top and a few female flowers further down.

Apple trees have male and female parts in the same flower. Insects carry the pollen to the female parts.

FRUITS

Oak acorns have a large store of food for the young seedlings. They just drop to the ground.

The winged seeds of the sycamore grow in pairs and spin down to the ground in the wind.

The fruits of the plane are spiky bobbles and hang on the tree all winter.

The shiny brown nuts of the beech grow in pairs inside a spiny husk.

CONES

Left: The long cones of spruce hang down to shake out the winged seeds which flutter to the ground.

Right: The noble fir has the largest cone of all. It stands upright on the twig. The bract scales stick out between the scales of the cone.

Left: Larch cones are small rosettes growing all round the twigs. They open to release winged seeds.

Right: Cypresses have small, round cones. This Monterey cypress cone is larger than that of most cypresses.

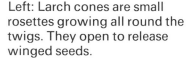

How a Tree Grows

Every year a tree grows taller and produces a new set of twigs so the crown of the tree expands upwards and outwards.

The trunk also grows outwards under the bark and that is why there are cracks and fissures in the bark of all but the youngest trees. Each kind of tree produces its own pattern of cracks and fissures (see page 4 for some examples). The bark pattern is quite a good way of recognizing trees in winter or when the leaves are too high to see clearly.

All this growth requires a lot of moisture from the soil, particularly in the spring when the tree grows most rapidly. By mid-summer it is growing more slowly and during this time the tree is storing up food for rapid growth in the next spring.

MEASURING HEIGHT

You can measure the height of a tree using a stick, a tape measure, and the help of a friend. Walk 27 paces away from the tree and ask your friend to hold a stick upright there. Go three more paces and look back at the tree, past the stick, from ground level.

Tell your friend to put his or her hand on the stick in line with where you see the top of the tree. Measure the distance from your friend's hand to the ground using the tape measure. Multiply this distance by ten to get the height of the tree in whatever units you measured the height of your friend's hand on the stick.

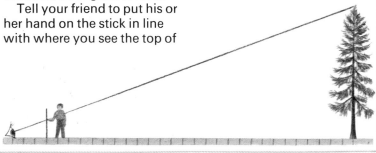

ESTIMATING AGE
Using Annual Rings

Every year, until a tree dies, it grows a new ring of wood all round the trunk and branches, just under the bark. When the tree is cut down, each year's ring can be seen. You can tell the age of the tree by counting the rings on the stump. The rings are not always evenly spaced apart. A larger distance between rings shows a good year's growth. A narrow distance shows less growth, perhaps due to cold weather or a shortage of rain.

The outer rings, called the sapwood, are alive and carry the tree's food, but the inner

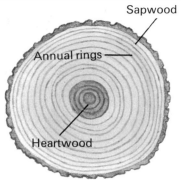

Sapwood

Annual rings

Heartwood

rings are dead and just provide support. They are usually much darker and are called the heartwood. This makes the best timber. Trees live a long time and are the oldest living things in the world.

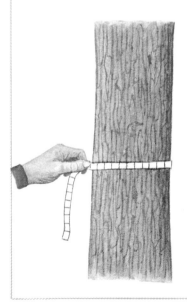

Using Girth

Because a tree adds a new ring of wood every year, the distance round the trunk – its girth – increases every year too. The girth can be used to estimate age without cutting down the tree.

Measure the girth 1·5 metres above the ground, and allow one year for every 25 mm. So a tree which is 2·5 metres in girth is about a hundred years old. However, if it is in a dense wood, it will have grown more slowly and will be nearer two hundred years old.

Other Things to Do

MAKING A BOOK OF TREES

There is a space in this book to record when and where you first spotted each kind of tree. You can also measure its girth and record its age. You may want to make a fuller record of the trees you see and include some not given in this book. As well as recording details about each tree, you can press and keep one of its leaves and make a rubbing of its bark. You can stick these in a book with perhaps a photograph of the tree.

Pressing Leaves

To dry a leaf, lay it flat between blotting paper or newpaper. Put a heavy weight, such as a pile of large books, on top for a few days. The leaf will then stay flat when it is stuck into a book. Write the name and place where you found it underneath.

Bark Rubbings

Every kind of tree has a different bark. Oak has a thick, fissured bark and beech has a much thinner, smooth bark. Getting to know the bark is a good way of identifying trees. To make a bark rubbing, tie a large piece of fairly thin paper on the tree. Rub over it with a wax crayon, being careful not to tear the paper. The bark pattern will then appear on the paper.

Finding Out More About Trees

Trees are important to our surroundings. They are attractive to look at and provide colour and shade in towns as well as in the countryside. They grow slowly and need to be carefully looked after. They are easily damaged, particularly when they are young. You can help to preserve trees and learn more about them by joining a club or society interested in trees. Some schools have tree clubs.

Information on trees can be obtained from the Tree Council, Agricultural House, Knightsbridge, London SW1X 7NJ which encourages tree-planting schemes for children, and from the Forestry Commission at 231 Corstorphine Road, Edinburgh EH12 7AT. You can also join either of these societies: Royal Forestry Society of England, Wales and Northern Ireland, 102 High Street, Tring HP23 4AH. This is open to everyone in England and Wales and arranges woodland meetings all over the country. The Royal Scottish Society, 18 Abercromby Place, Edinburgh EH3 6LB is the equivalent society in Scotland.

Coniferous Trees

You can recognize a conifer by its needle-like or scale-like leaves. Most conifers are evergreen and keep their leaves in winter, dropping them after three or four years. However, some broad-leafed trees, such as holly (see page 40) also keep their leaves in winter. So do not assume that an evergreen is a conifer, it is not necessarily the case. All conifers produce cones and these are also a useful clue in identifying the tree.

Conifers can grow in colder and drier regions than broad-leafed trees. Their thick, narrow leaves resist frost. You will find conifers growing much higher up a mountainside than most other trees.

Some conifers grow much faster than other trees. Spruce trees in particular are often grown in large plantations to provide a quick source of timber.

SCOTS PINE
Native
Leaves: grow in pairs, 6 cm long.
The Scots pine grows in the Scottish Highlands and on sandy heaths in southern England. The bark on the upper trunk and branches is red. Look for the bluish-green leaves and for the cones which are knobbly and conical.

DATE _____

PLACE _____

GIRTH _____

NORWAY SPRUCE

European

Leaves: single, 2 cm long.
This is the traditional Christmas tree. It is tall and triangular with dark green leaves. The light brown cigar-shaped cones hang down. The needles are sharp and the bark is light brown.

Look too for the Sitka spruce. It has a scaly, grey bark and small cones with papery scales.

DATE _____

PLACE _____

GIRTH _____

CORSICAN PINE

European

Leaves: grow in pairs, 12 cm long.
The Corsican pine has blacker bark with longer, coarser and darker needles. The Austrian pine is very similar. They both have much larger, more rounded cones than the Scots pine. They grow well in eastern Britain where Corsican pine is the main timber tree.

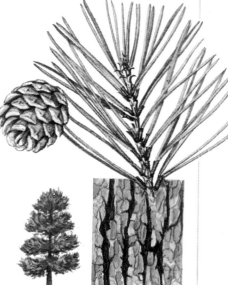

DATE _____ _____

PLACE _____

GIRTH _____

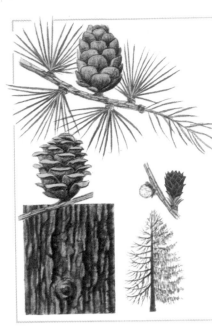

EUROPEAN LARCH
European
Leaves: single on young twigs, in rosettes on older shoots; 3 cm long.
This tall, narrow tree has fine, horizontal branches and a straight stem. The light green leaves are on yellow twigs. The female flowers are red and the male flowers yellow. The cones are egg-shaped.

DATE _____

PLACE _____

GIRTH _____

GRAND FIR
North American
Leaves: single, notched at tip, 1·5–2·5 cm long.
This is a tall tree, clothed to the ground with dark branches. The leaves are flattened to either side of the twigs and vary in length. The young bark is smooth and has sweet-smelling resin blisters. The cones stand upright and break up to release the seeds.

DATE _____

PLACE _____

GIRTH _____

16

DOUGLAS FIR
North American
Leaves: single needles,
3 cm long.
This very tall tree has long branches, and soft needles that smell sweetly. The buds are copper-brown and pointed, like those of beech. The female flowers are dark red before they turn to light brown, hanging cones with long bracts between the scales.

DATE _____

PLACE _____

GIRTH _____

NOBLE FIR
North American
Leaves: single, 1·5–2·5 cm.
This is a mountain tree with blue-green leaves and grey bark. The yellow flowers turn into large, upright cones on the top branches. The cones have down-turned bracts which stick out between the scales. The cones fall apart at the first frost and release the seeds.

DATE _____

PLACE _____

GIRTH _____

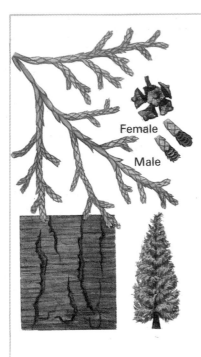

LAWSON CYPRESS
North American
Leaves: 2 mm long, enclosing small twigs.

This medium-sized tree is found mainly in gardens. The small scale-like leaves are dark green above and have white lines on the underside. In spring there are numerous little red male flowers and dark green female flowers. Later in the year, small, round cones appear. The bark is soft and smooth.

Many varieties with different shapes and colours have been cultivated and grow well in British gardens. The leaves can vary from blue-grey to yellow, golden or very dark green. Some varieties are narrow and tall, others are broad, and many are grown as dwarf trees.

Female

Male

DATE _____

PLACE _____

GIRTH _____

Western red cedar

'Tamariscifolia'   'Lutea'   'Green pillar' 'Ellwoodii'   'Lanei'   'Erecta'

18

LEYLAND CYPRESS

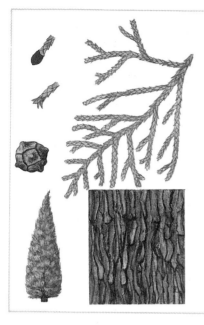

A native hybrid
Leaves: 2 mm long,
enclosing small twigs.
This tall, very fast-growing
tree is usually found in
gardens. It is often used for
hedges as it quickly forms a
thick screen. The leaves are
very like those of the Lawson
cypress and they cover the
tree right down to the ground
It seldom forms cones.

DATE _____

PLACE _____

GIRTH _____

MONTEREY CYPRESS

North American
Leaves: 1 mm long,
enclosing small twigs.
This narrow tree, when
young, gets a broad, flat top
as it ages. The very small,
scale-like leaves cover the
twigs. Look for the cones
which are large, rounded and
lumpy. The tree thrives in salt
winds and so is often planted
on the coast to provide
shelter.

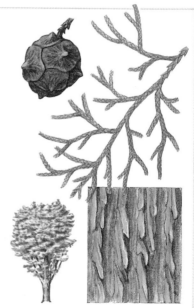

DATE _____

PLACE _____

GIRTH _____

19

COAST REDWOOD

North American
Leaves: 2 mm long.
This very tall tree grows well in Britain. In its native home of California, there is one which is 112 metres tall. It is the tallest tree in the world. Coast redwoods live to a great age and many in California are 2500 years old.

The dark green leaves have sharp tips. They are almost white on the underside. The attractive red bark is soft and very thick. It protects the trees in California from forest fires, which is probably why they grow to such a great age there. The small cones grow

at the ends of the twigs.

In Britain, Coast redwood has only been used as an ornamental tree, but it is common in parks and large gardens. The tallest in Britain is one of 40 metres at Taymouth Castle in Perthshire. Near Welshpool in Powys there are 36 trees which are now well over 100 years old.

Male

Female

DATE _____

PLACE _____

GIRTH _____

WELLINGTONIA
North American
Leaves: 6 mm long,
enclosing twigs.
This tall redwood has a spire-like top, which is often killed by lightning. The dark green, scale-like leaves have a curved tip. The large, rounded cones are tough and corky. The dull brown bark is thick and soft. In California, some trees are 3400 years old.

DATE _____

PLACE _____

GIRTH _____

DAWN REDWOOD
Chinese
Leaves: single and flat,
2 cm long.
This tree was only known as a fossil until living specimens were found in China in 1941. The soft leaves are light green. Its bark is soft and stringy on the deeply ridged trunk. It likes moist ground and grows easily from cuttings. It is now quite common in gardens.

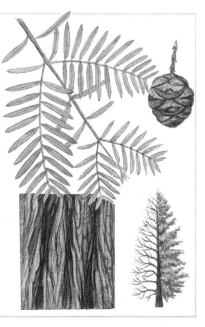

DATE _____

PLACE _____

GIRTH _____

ATLAS AND LEBANON CEDARS

Mediterranean
Leaves: single and in rosettes; about 3 cm long. Atlas and Lebanon cedars are very alike with heavy, spreading branches which make a broad, open top. Cedars flower in the autumn, producing a lot of yellow pollen. Their fat, barrel-shaped cones sit upright on the branches.

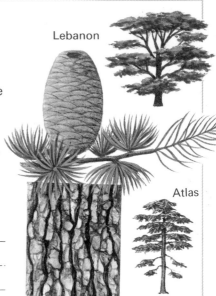

Lebanon

Atlas

DATE _____

PLACE _____.

GIRTH _____

DEODAR CEDAR

Himalayan
Leaves: single and in rosettes; about 3 cm long. The Deodor is similar to the other cedars, except that it is narrower in shape and the ends of its branches and its leading shoot hangs down.

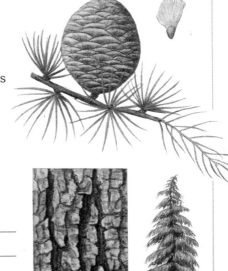

DATE _____

PLACE _____

GIRTH _____

22

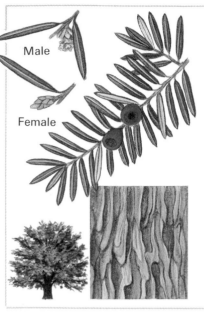

YEW
Native
Leaves: single, 3 cm long, sharply pointed.
A small, long-lived tree, which grows mainly on chalky soils. The **poisonous** leaves are dark green above and lighter below. Look for the separate male and female trees. The male tree has yellow flowers in spring, and the female has **poisonous** red berries in autumn. Yew makes a dense hedge.

DATE _____

PLACE _____

GIRTH _____

MONKEY PUZZLE
South American
Leaves: single, 4 cm long, very sharply pointed.
This is a regularly shaped tree with few branches. The large, flat, spiny leaves cover the branches and stem, making the tree impossible to climb and giving it its name. The female trees sometimes produce large brown cones. The trunk is wrinkled and grey, like an elephant's skin.

DATE _____

PLACE _____

GIRTH _____

Broad-leafed Trees

Broad-leafed trees, as their name implies, have larger, flatter leaves than conifers. Most broad-leafed trees drop their leaves in autumn. As the leaves begin to dry up and die on the tree, they may change from green to gold, to orange, red or brown before they fall. By dropping their leaves, the more sensitive broad-leafed trees can withstand the hard weather of winter. Not only the shape of the leaf, but the flowers, fruit and shape of the tree all provide useful clues to its identity.

Broad-leafed trees grow all over the country, but some like a particular kind of soil and will be very common in those areas which provide it. There are many beech woods in southern England, while only the rowan and birch can share with the conifers the rugged climate of parts of northern Scotland.

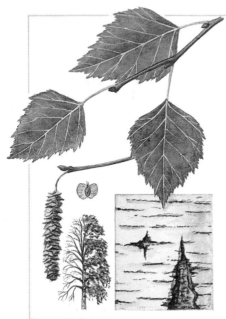

BIRCH
Native
Leaves: alternate, 6 cm long. A small tree that grows all over the country, but particularly on dry soils and mountains. The triangular leaves are bright green with large teeth. Look for the catkin flowers in early spring. They shed their seed in the following winter. The bark is often silvery-white.

DATE _____

PLACE _____

GIRTH _____

BEECH
Native
Leaves: alternate, 8–10 cm.
This tall tree has a silvery-grey
trunk. It grows particularly
well on chalk soils in south-
eastern England. The oval
leaves have wavy edges and
parallel veins, and are downy
in spring. The long buds and
triangular nuts are both rich
brown. The flowers are small.

DATE _____

PLACE _____

GIRTH _____

HORNBEAM
Native
Leaves: alternate, 4–10 cm.
A small tree with a rounded
crown. It is common only in
the south-east of Britain. The
oval leaves are pointed, with
double teeth on the edge and
parallel veins. Birds and
squirrels like the tiny nuts
which are held in a leafy,
three-lobed bract. The
flowers are small catkins.

DATE _____

PLACE _____

GIRTH _____

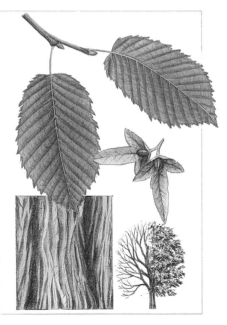

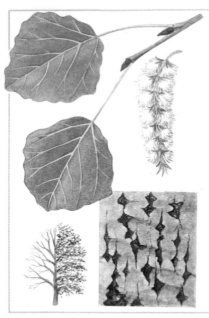

ASPEN
Native
Leaves: alternate, 4–6 cm.
This small tree is not common, but occurs all over the country. The rounded leaves quiver in the wind due to their flattened stalks. The silvery bark has black diamonds. The long male and female catkins grow on different trees, the females shedding woolly seeds in May.

DATE _____

PLACE _____

GIRTH _____

BLACK POPLAR
Native
Leaves: alternate, 5–8 cm.
A large tree of the lowlands. The large yellowish-green leaves are pointed with small teeth on their edges. The large buds are pointed and chestnut brown. The grey bark is deeply furrowed. The well-known Lombardy poplar is a form of the black poplar with a narrow crown.

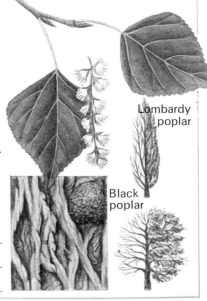

Lombardy poplar

Black poplar

DATE _____

PLACE _____

GIRTH _____

WHITE POPLAR
European
Leaves: alternate, 9 cm.
The white poplar has greenish-white bark with large black diamonds on it. The red male and green female catkins are long and grow on separate trees. The female ones turn into fluffy white seeds. The similar grey poplar is thought to be a cross between aspen and white poplar.

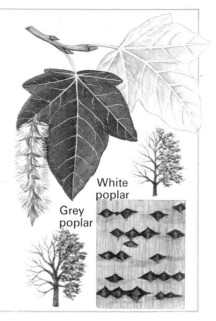

White poplar

Grey poplar

DATE _____

PLACE _____

GIRTH _____

BALSAM POPLAR
North American
Leaves: alternate, 10–30 cm.
This is a fast-growing tree. In spring its sticky buds are sweet-smelling. They are chestnut brown and pointed. The underside of its large, triangular leaves are silvery and metallic looking. The red male catkins grow on separate trees from the green female catkins. They produce fluffy white seeds in May.

DATE _____

PLACE _____

GIRTH _____

27

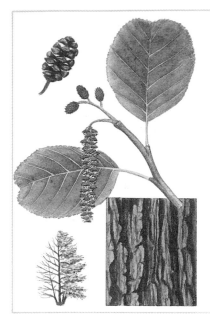

ALDER
Native
Leaves: alternate, 4–10 cm.
A small tree that grows near water. Look for the rounded leaves with a notched tip or the stalked buds. The orange-brown male catkins hang down in spring. The small female catkins are like knobs on the same tree. They turn into woody 'cones' which drop their seeds into the water to scatter them.

DATE _____

PLACE _____

GIRTH _____

GOAT WILLOW
Native
Leaves: alternate, 5–10 cm.
This very small tree more often grows as a shrub with several stems. The leathery oval leaves are dark green above and woolly-grey underneath. In early spring the grey 'pussy' catkins give the tree its country name of 'pussy' willow. On male trees they later turn yellow and on females green.

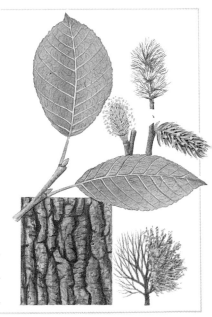

DATE _____

PLACE _____

GIRTH _____

Female   Male

WHITE WILLOW
Native
Leaves: alternate,
up to 12 cm.
This small tree is found along streams and in damp woods. Its long, thin leaves have silvery hairs underneath. The buds lie close to the yellow twigs. The male and female catkins grow on separate trees. The bark is rough. Cricket bats are made from the soft and resilient wood.

DATE _____

PLACE _____

GIRTH _____

WEEPING WILLOW
Leaves: alternate,
up to 12 cm.
There are several trees known as weeping willow. They all have long, drooping twigs hanging down almost to the ground. The older weeping willows have brown twigs, but several planted nowadays have yellow twigs. All willows like moisture and are often planted by water.

DATE _____

PLACE _____

GIRTH _____

29

WILD CHERRY
Native
Leaves: alternate, 10 cm.
This medium-sized tree is easy to spot in spring by its white flowers. The long, toothed leaves have two lumpy glands at the base. The dark red fruits are sour but birds and squirrels like them. The bark is a shiny red-brown with horizontal bands.

DATE _____

PLACE _____

GIRTH _____

BIRD CHERRY
Native
Leaves: alternate, 8 cm.
This small tree is often seen growing in hedges. The small white flowers hang down in long bunches in spring. Birds like the small, black, bitter fruits. The leaves are smaller and rounder than those of the wild cherry. The bark is black coloured and rough with fine ridges.

DATE _____

PLACE _____

GIRTH _____

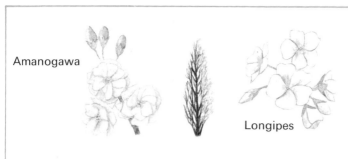

Amanogawa

Longipes

Kanzan

JAPANESE CHERRY
Chinese

Leaves: alternate, 10–15 cm. The ornamental flowering cherries that you see growing in gardens are mostly varieties of the Japanese cherry. This tree has been cultivated for a very long time in Japan, and many different and attractive forms of it have been developed. They all have a rich red and shiny bark with many horizontal bands round the stems.

The shapes vary. Some are spreading or weeeping, others are narrow and upright. The flowers also vary greatly, but the most popular are pink. Each variety has its own name. The most common one is probably 'Kanzan' with double pink flowers. It is very popular in suburban gardens.

DATE _____

PLACE _____

GIRTH _____

31

CRAB APPLE
Native
Leaves: alternate, 7–8 cm.
You may occasionally see this small tree growing wild, but usually because it has grown from the pips in a discarded apple core. It has rounded leaves with small teeth on the edges and a rounded tip. The large flowers are pinkish-white. They turn into small green apples which are too sour for us to eat, although horses and many wild animals like them.

Orchard apples have large edible fruit. They have been developed from the wild crab apple. They all have different names and are grown for different purposes, such as eating, cooking, and good winter storage.

DATE _____

PLACE _____

GIRTH _____

Crab Apple

Golden Delicious

Granny Smith

Discovery

SWEET CHESTNUT
Mediterranean
Leaves: alternate, 15–20 cm.
This large tree may live a long time. It then has a great girth and is often three or four hundred years old. The older the tree the greater the twist to the long spiral furrows in the bark. These twist to the left or to the right.

The very long leaves have large, saw-like teeth. The flowers are long too, and the tassel-like catkins contain the male and female flowers together.

The fruits have spiny green shells with two or three brown nuts inside. They are very popular with squirrels. We can roast and eat them too, although they seldom grow large enough for this in Britain.

The strong wood of sweet chestnut is very like oak and is easily mistaken for it. Many so-called oak beams in old houses are often really sweet chestnut timber.

DATE _____

PLACE _____

GIRTH _____

COMMON LIME

A natural hybrid of large-
and small-leafed limes,
probably introduced
Leaves: alternate, 5–10 cm.
This is the tallest broad-
leafed tree in Britain. It is
often planted in avenues and
is easy to spot from its
downward arching branches.

Its leaves are heart-shaped
and have triangular teeth.
Certain insects, called aphids,
often feed on the sap of the
leaves. When this is partly
digested it becomes sticky
and drips on to the pavement
or cars parked underneath.
This can be a nuisance when
the trees are planted in towns.

Other kinds of lime are
attacked by these insects less
often.

Several sweet-smelling
flowers grow on a leafy bract.
Bees are attracted to their
nectar, and so lime trees are
popular with bee-keepers.
The flowers turn into small,
rounded fruits.

The bark has fine ridges.
The wood is light with a fine
grain and is used to make
musical instruments.

DATE _____

PLACE _____

GIRTH _____

SMALL-LEAFED LIME
Native
Leaves: alternate, 4–6 cm.
This tree grows to about half the height of the common lime. Its leaves are smaller and are less heart-shaped. They are not often attacked by leaf-sucking insects. There are seven or eight yellow flowers on each bract. Look for the fruits which are not ribbed like those of other limes.

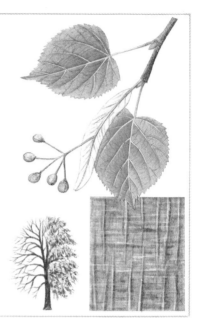

DATE _____

PLACE _____

GIRTH _____

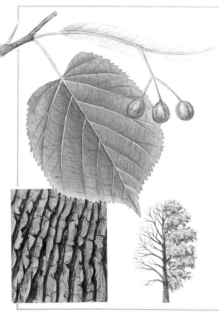

LARGE-LEAFED LIME
Probably native
Leaves: alternate, up to 15 cm.
This tree is larger than the small-leafed lime, but smaller than the common lime. It has much larger, heart-shaped leaves. There are only three or four flowers on each bract. They come out before those of other limes, and so provide early food for bees.

DATE _____

PLACE _____

GIRTH _____

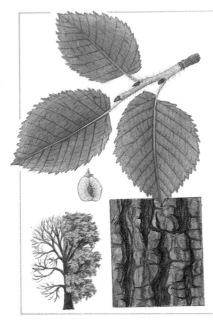

FIELD ELM
European, not native
Leaves: alternate, 7 cm.
This tall tree used to be common in the hedgerows and fields of southern England, but many elms have now been destroyed by Dutch elm disease. The leaves have an unequal base, reaching farther down the leaf stalk on one side than the other. Its many small flowers make the whole tree look purplish in spring.

DATE _____

PLACE _____

GIRTH _____

WYCH ELM
Native
Leaves: alternate, 15 cm.
The wych elm is more rounded than the field elm and its long-pointed leaves are about twice the size. This hardy tree is more common in the north. Most other elms grow mainly from suckers, but wych elm usually grows from seed. This makes it less liable to the fatal Dutch elm disease.

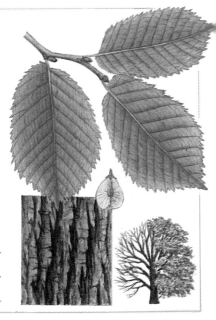

DATE _____

PLACE _____

GIRTH _____

OAK
Native

Leaves: alternate, 8–12 cm. When fully grown, this massive tree with its heavy branches produces excellent timber. Its leaves are lobed. The bark is rough and fissured. The small male and female flowers appear on the same tree in May. The seed is a large acorn which is a popular food for birds and animals.

Oak forests covered much of Britain before the land began to be cleared for farming 9000 years ago. At first the timber would have been used for firewood, but later it became important for building because it is so strong. The bark was used for tanning (curing) leather. When large wooden ships were built, oak was the most suitable timber for them. It was, and still is, a valuable timber for making furniture, but it grows more slowly than other trees.

DATE _____

PLACE _____

GIRTH _____

LONDON PLANE

Native
Leaves: alternate, 15 cm.
This large tree is often seen in city parks and streets. The old bark flakes off in large plates, leaving yellow patches of clean fresh bark. Look for the five-lobed leaves. The rounded male and female flowers grow on the same tree. The hanging spiky fruits are easy to see on the bare trees in winter.

DATE _____

PLACE _____

GIRTH _____

NORWAY MAPLE

European, now naturalized
Leaves: opposite, 12 cm.
The Norway maple is rather smaller than the sycamore and is more lightly branched. Its leaves are similar but the tips of the lobes are much more pointed. The yellow flowers come out in early spring before the leaves. They provide food for bees when there is little else available.

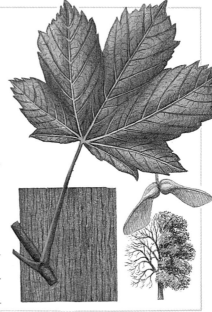

DATE _____

PLACE _____

GIRTH _____

SYCAMORE
European, now naturalized
Leaves: opposite, 18 cm.
This large, rounded tree
grows everywhere, even on
windy coasts and mountains.
The hand-shaped leaves are
sometimes purple on the
underside. Greenish-yellow
flowers appear with the
leaves. They produce paired,
winged seeds that flutter to
the ground in autumn.

DATE _____

PLACE _____

GIRTH _____

FIELD MAPLE
Native
Leaves: opposite, 8 cm.
This small hedgerow tree
grows mainly on chalk soils in
southern England. The small
leaves have rounded lobes.
The yellowish-green flowers
come out with the leaves. The
wings of the small, paired
seeds are almost in a straight
line. The twigs often have
corky 'wings'. The bark is
orange-grey.

DATE _____

PLACE _____

GIRTH _____

39

HOLLY
Native
Leaves: alternate, 6–8 cm.
A small tree shaped like a pyramid. It is usually seen in hedges or as a shrub in woods. Its glossy, prickly leaves are evergreen. The white female and male flowers grow on separate trees. The female trees bear the bright red berries that attract birds. The bark is smooth and grey.

DATE _____

PLACE _____

GIRTH _____

HAWTHORN
Native
Leaves: alternate, 4–7 cm.
Hawthorn is really a small tree, but is often grown in hedges because of its sharp thorns. Its small leaves are deeply lobed. It has many showy white flowers in spring. They turn to deep red berries which are eaten by birds. The brown bark is scaly.

DATE _____

PLACF _____

GIRTH _____

WHITEBEAM

Native in southern England
Leaves: alternate, 5–10 cm.
This small tree grows on chalk soils, and is often planted in streets. The undersides of the leaves are covered with dense white hairs, the upper sides are grey-green. It has large heads of white flowers in spring which turn to clusters of red berries in autumn. The bark is smooth and grey.

DATE _____

PLACE _____

GIRTH _____

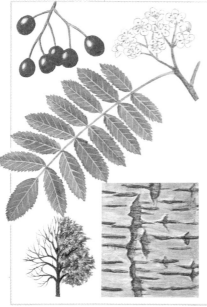

MOUNTAIN ASH (ROWAN)

Native
Leaves: alternate, 22 cm.
A small, mountain tree with light branches. It is often planted on roadsides. The leaves are divided into many small leaflets. The clustered creamy white flowers of spring turn to red berries by late summer and are very popular with birds. The bark is smooth and grey.

DATE _____

PLACE _____

GIRTH _____

WALNUT
Southern European and
Asian
Leaves: alternate, up to
18 cm.
This large spreading tree is
never found in woods but is
often planted near farm
houses. The leaves come late
in spring and are bronze
before turning green. They
are divided into several
rounded leaflets. The edible
nuts inside the green fruit
seldom get large enough in
Britain to eat.

DATE _____

PLACE _____

GIRTH _____

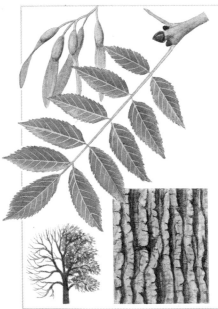

ASH
Native
Leaves: opposite, 20–30 cm.
This tall tree has few
branches and grey, furrowed
bark. The leaves are divided
into many leaflets. The purple
male and female flowers
come out before the leaves,
giving the tree a purplish
colour. Look for the bunches
of single winged seeds which
hang on the tree from mid-
summer all through winter.

DATE _____

PLACE _____

GIRTH _____

FALSE ACACIA (ROBINIA)

North American
Leaves: alternate, 15–20 cm.
Grows as a small garden tree in the south of England. The leaves are divided into many rounded leaflets. In a warm summer, long hanging clusters of white pea-like flowers cover the tree and turn into seeds in pods in autumn. The brown bark is rough and deeply furrowed. The twigs have sharp spines.

DATE _____

PLACE _____

GIRTH _____

LABURNUM

Southern European
Leaves: alternate, 2·5–7·5 cm.
A small, ornamental garden tree. The leaves are divided into three leaflets. Look for the pea-like yellow flowers which hang in tassels and cover the tree in spring. The small black seeds in the hanging pods are **poisonous** and must never be eaten.

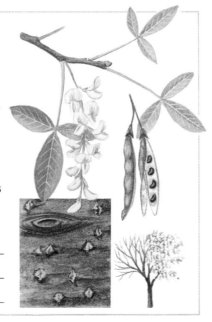

DATE _____

PLACE _____

GIRTH _____

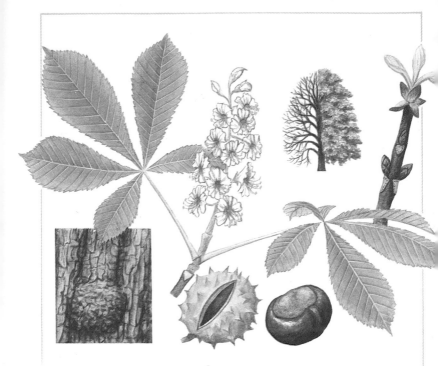

HORSE CHESTNUT

Mediterranean

Leaves: opposite, 50 cm.

This large tree is named after the leaf scars, left when the leaves fall. They are shaped like horse-shoes and you can easily see them on the twigs in winter. The ends of the veins that ran into the leaf look like the nails in a horse-shoe.

Horse chestnuts have downward arching branches, and are often planted in parks and avenues. The leaf is divided into five or seven large leaflets, which spread out like the fingers of a hand. The showy white or red flowers look like candles on the tree in spring.

The shiny brown conkers are contained in a spiky, green fruit and are collected by children to play the game of conkers. The brown bark flakes off in thin plates.

DATE _____

PLACE _____

GIRTH _____

Unusual Trees

There are many botanical gardens in Britain which grow foreign and unusual trees, and they are always interesting to visit. Even in large parks and gardens you will probably find some unusual trees which have been specially planted. Only a small selection is shown here.

The tulip tree and the Indian bean are broad-leafed trees, but the maidenhair is neither a conifer nor a broadleaf. It is more closely related to ferns and gets its name from its leaves which are like those of the maidenhair fern.

Palms also form a quite separate group. They do not grow a new ring of wood round their trunks each year (see page 11). Most palms in Britain are only able to grow on the south or west coasts where the Gulf Stream provides a mild, wet climate which protects them from frost.

MAIDENHAIR TREE
Chinese
Leaves: alternate, 12 cm.
This unusual tree grows only in botanical gardens and parks now. It first appeared 200 million years ago, long before any other kind of tree alive today. It survived in some Chinese temple gardens and grows well in southern Britain. Look for the fan-shaped leaves which are quite unlike any other.

DATE _____

PLACE _____

GIRTH _____

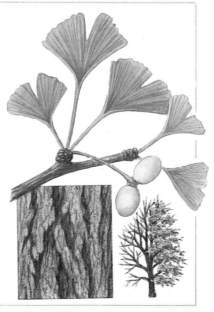

TULIP TREE
North American
Leaves: alternate, 10–15 cm.
This tall, narrow tree grows only in parks and gardens. Its leaf is unusual because it has four points but lacks a tip. In a good summer in southern England, it produces large creamy-green, tulip-like flowers. The fruit is like a brown bud with long, winged seeds.

DATE _____

PLACE _____

GIRTH _____

INDIAN BEAN
North American
Leaves: opposite, sometimes, in threes, 25 cm.
You can see this small, rounded tree in parks and gardens. The heart-shaped leaves do not appear until June. The white flowers are flecked with purple in an upright head. The seeds grow in long hanging pods that remain on the tree all winter.

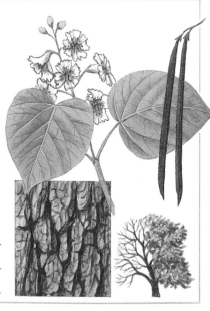

DATE _____

PLACE _____

GIRTH _____